HOME BUYING DECODED:

FROM CLUELESS TO CONFIDENT

16 Home Buying Rules No One Will Tell You

HOME BUYING DECODED:
FROM CLUELESS TO CONFIDENT

16 Home Buying Rules No One Will Tell You

Sashikant Barik

Sheikh Mairajul Haque

Worldwide Published by

Pendown Press

PENDOWN PRESS LLP
An ISO 9001 & ISO 14001 Certified Co.,
Regd. Office: 3767A, Kanhaiya Nagar,
Tri Nagar, Delhi-110035
Ph.: 8130886000, 9650072927
E-mail: info@pendownpress.com
Branch Office: 1A/2A, 20, Hari Sadan, Ansari Road,
Daryaganj, New Delhi-110002
Ph.: 011-45794768
Website: PendownPress.com

Edition: 2025

ISBN: 978-93-6338-389-0

Layout and Cover Designed by Pendown Graphics Team
Printed and Bound in India by Thomson Press India Ltd.

Home Buying Decoded: From Clueless to Confident

(16 Home Buying Rules No One Will Tell You)

"This book saved me from making a `5 lakh mistake! I was about to buy a property without checking the legal paperwork properly. The checklists and step-by-step approach helped me make a smarter decision, and now I own a home I truly love!"

— Rohan Mehta, First-Time Homebuyer

"I thought buying a home would be stressful, but this book made it easy." From understanding home loans to negotiating with the builder, every tip in here was a game-changer. I walked into my home-buying journey with confidence, and I couldn't be happier with my decision.

— Aditi Sharma, IT Professional

"I wish I had this book when I bought my first home." I made so many mistakes back then—hidden costs, bad financing, and zero negotiation skills. This book teaches everything a homebuyer needs to know in a simple, practical way. I'll be recommending it to all my friends!

— Vikram Rao, Real Estate Investor

"Straightforward, practical, and full of real-world insights." I followed the advice on down payments, home loans, and possession walkthroughs—and it saved me from unexpected costs. Every homebuyer in India needs to read this before making a decision!

— Pooja Nair, Marketing Executive

"The ultimate home-buying playbook!" I had no idea what to expect when buying my first home. This book broke down the entire process—no jargon, no fluff, just practical advice. It gave me clarity, confidence, and a solid game plan.

— Raj Malhotra, Entrepreneur

Table of Contents

SECTION 1: THE PRE-GAME PLAN – HOW TO GET READY FOR HOMEOWNERSHIP

SECTION 2: FINANCING & CLOSING LIKE A PRO

THE ULTIMATE HOME-BUYING CHECKLIST

- Pre-Purchase Checklist (Are You Actually Ready to Buy?)
- House Hunting Checklist (Finding the Right Property)
- Legal & Paperwork Checklist (The Must-Have Documents)
- Financial Checklist (Avoid Hidden Money Traps)
- Closing & Move-In Checklist (Final Step Before You Celebrate!)

FINAL THOUGHTS

- Home Buying is a Power Move – If Done Right
- The Real Value of Owning a Home
- Avoiding Buyer's Remorse & Owning It Like a Pro
- The Next Step is Yours

FOREWORD

The Home You Choose Today Shapes Your Tomorrow

A home is more than just walls and a roof — it's where your life unfolds. It's where memories are made, dreams take shape, and your future finds stability. As an architect, I've seen firsthand how homeownership changes lives, giving people not just a place to live but a foundation to grow.

Yet, for many professionals, buying a home can feel overwhelming. The questions, the paperwork, the financial decisions — it's easy to keep waiting for the "right time." But time moves, markets shift, and waiting too long often means spending years paying rent — helping someone else build their wealth instead of your own.

This book is here to change that.

Why Trust This Book?

I've worked closely with Sashikant and Mairaj, and if there's one thing I can say with certainty — it's that they genuinely care about home buyers. They don't just build homes; they **understand the journey buyers go through, the financial commitments involved, and the challenges that often lead to costly mistakes.**

Through years of experience, they've guided thousands of people—first-time buyers, families, and investors—toward making informed, confident decisions. And that's exactly what this book will do for you.

This is not just a guide; it's a **step-by-step roadmap to home buying, designed to simplify the process, clear doubts, and give you the confidence to make one of the biggest decisions of your life.**

By the last page, you won't just understand how to buy a home — you'll be ready to **own your future.**

Hafeez Contractor
Architect & Urban Planner

MEET YOUR GUIDES:
OUR STORY

**From Channel Partners to Developers —
Why We Wrote This Book**

Before we built homes, designed spaces, and shaped neighborhoods, we were on the other side of the table—helping buyers navigate the complexities of real estate.

As channel partners, we worked with hundreds—sometimes thousands—of buyers every month. We saw the excitement, the hesitation, the financial anxieties, and the overwhelming confusion that came with purchasing a home. We sat through negotiations, answered endless questions, and witnessed firsthand the struggles people faced when making one of the biggest decisions of their lives.

We didn't just observe real estate—we **lived it** through the eyes of homebuyers.

And that's exactly what makes this book different.

Most real estate advice comes from banks, brokers, or developers who have never actually sat down with buyers to truly understand their concerns. But we have. We know the fears, the doubts, the common mistakes, and the **"I wish someone had told me this earlier"** moments.

Now, as developers, we've taken everything we've learned and applied it to **create homes that solve real problems**—and to **write this book** so you can buy with confidence.

From Engineers to Real Estate Experts — A Journey Built on Experience

Like most young professionals, we started our careers in engineering. We were trained to **solve problems, think logically, and plan with precision**. But when we transitioned into real estate, we quickly realized something important:

Buying a home isn't just a financial decision—it's an emotional one.

It's about **security, pride, and long-term growth**. But the process of buying a home? That's where most people struggle.

During our years working directly with buyers, we saw:

- **Misinformation leading to costly mistakes.** Many families invested their life savings into properties that weren't the right fit for them.
- **Buyers stuck in "analysis paralysis."** With too much information and too many options, people hesitated for years and missed out on great opportunities.

We knew there had to be a better way.

So when we transitioned from being advisors to developers, we made a commitment:

√ **To build homes that provide real value.**

√ **To be upfront and honest about the buying process.**

√ **To empower buyers with the knowledge to make informed decisions—without stress or uncertainty.**

The Lessons We Learned (So You Don't Have To)

Even with years of industry experience, stepping into real estate development came with its own learning curve. We made mistakes, learned valuable lessons, and gained a **deep understanding of what homebuyers truly need.**

Here are some of the most important things we've learned:

- **Not all homes are built the same.** Fancy brochures don't guarantee high-quality construction. Always verify the materials and builder's track record.

- **Home loans aren't always as simple as they seem.** What's "approved" isn't always what's best for you. Understanding interest rates and repayment structures is crucial.

- **The fine print matters.** Small clauses in real estate contracts can lead to unexpected costs down the line. Read every detail before signing.

- **The best deals aren't just about price—they're about value.** A lower price doesn't always mean a smarter investment. Location, amenities, the builder's reputation, and long-term appreciation potential matter just as much.

Why We Wrote This Book

Most people struggle with home buying **not because they lack money—but because they lack the right information.** And unfortunately, **misinformation is everywhere.**

We've seen buyers:

- Overpaying for properties because they didn't negotiate.
- Walking away from great homes out of fear of making a wrong decision.
- Getting caught in confusing legalities and hidden costs they weren't prepared for.

And we didn't want that to happen to you.

That's why we wrote this book—so you can navigate the home-buying process **with clarity, confidence, and the right knowledge.**

This book will give you:

√ **A playbook for identifying a great deal (and walking away from a bad one).**

√ **Negotiation strategies that can save you lakhs.**

√ **A clear understanding of home loans, contracts, and financial planning.**

√ **A step-by-step roadmap to buying smart and securing your future.**

This isn't just another real estate book filled with generic advice. **This is the guide we wish existed when we first started.**

So whether you're buying your **first home, upgrading to your dream home, or thinking about real estate investment**, this book will help you make the best possible decision—**without stress, doubt, or unnecessary delays.**

Because buying a home isn't just about where you live.

It's about owning your future.

And we're here to help you do it right.

SECTION 1:

THE PRE-GAME PLAN: HOW TO GET READY FOR HOMEOWNERSHIP**

Think You're Ready to Buy? Let's Make Sure.

So, you've decided it's time to buy a home. Maybe your rent keeps going up. Maybe you're ready to invest in something that's yours. Or maybe it just feels like the next big step in your life.

Either way, **this is an exciting milestone.** But before you start picturing your dream home, let's make sure you're set up for success.

Buying a home isn't just about finding a great property—it's about **being financially and mentally prepared** so that the process is smooth and stress-free. The more prepared you are, the more confident you'll feel in making the right decision.

Here's what this section will help you with:

√ **Renting vs. Buying**—Understanding why owning a home builds long-term security and wealth.

√ **How to calculate what you can comfortably afford**—So you can move forward with confidence.

√ **The full cost of homeownership**—Beyond just the EMI, so you know exactly what to expect.

√ **The down payment game**—How to plan for it in a way that works for you.

By the end of this section, you'll have **a clear, confident strategy** for buying a home. No second-guessing, no surprises—just smart, informed decisions that set you up for a **secure, successful** future as a homeowner.

Chapter - 1

THE SMART PERSON'S GUIDE TO BUYING A HOME (WITHOUT LOSING YOUR MIND)

So, You Want to Buy a Home?

You're standing at one of the biggest financial decisions of your life: **To buy or not to buy?**

Friends, family, and self-proclaimed financial "experts" all have opinions:

√ "Buying is too expensive!"

√ "Renting is smarter!"

√ "You'll be in debt forever!"

√ "Just buy something before prices go up again!"

Let's set the record straight—**most people have NO CLUE what they're talking about.**

And here's the reality: **Those who own homes quietly build wealth, while renters keep debating whether buying makes sense.**

Homeownership isn't just about having a place to live—it's about **security, stability, and smart financial growth.**

Renting vs. Buying: Where Does Your Money Actually Go?

"Renting is like paying for a hotel room every month— but at the end of the year, you still don't own the building."

Here's what's happening when you rent:

√ Your landlord's property appreciates in value while you keep paying.

√ Your rent increases every year, while you get nothing in return.

√ You have zero tax benefits—while homeowners enjoy deductions on home loans.

√ You can't renovate, modify, or invest in a place that's truly yours.

After **10 years of renting**, you have spent **lakhs—and own nothing.**

After **10 years of homeownership**, you have built **equity in a real asset** that could be worth double its original price.

√ **Fact:** On average, people in India spend over ₹ 50 lakh on rent over 10 years without realizing it.

(Source: Economic Times Real Estate Report, 2023)

The "It's Smarter to Rent" Myth

You've probably heard:

"If you rent and invest the difference, you'll be better off financially."

But let's be real—how many people actually **invest the difference?**

- Most renters spend extra money on lifestyle expenses rather than investments.
- Meanwhile, **homeowners see their property value increase over time.**

Think about it: Have you ever met someone who said, **"I rented for 20 years, and now I'm rich!"**? Exactly.

But how many people have you seen say, **"I bought a home years ago, and now it's worth double"**? That's not a coincidence.

"But Buying a Home is Too Expensive!"

You know what else is expensive?

Paying rent forever and owning nothing.

Yes, homeownership comes with responsibilities. But the biggest mistake you can make is **waiting too long.**

Here's what happens when you delay:

- **Property values rise over time**—what seems expensive today will seem like a steal in five years.
- **Interest rates fluctuate**—and usually not in your favor.
- **Your expenses increase with inflation**—but a home is a long-term financial safety net.

The best time to buy a home? Yesterday.

The second-best time? Right now.

How to Buy Smart (And Avoid Costly Mistakes)

Before you jump in, let's make sure you're **making the right moves.**

√ **Buy when it's right for YOU.** Don't let family or social pressure rush your decision.

√ **Ignore bad financial advice.** Always take advice from people who actually own real estate.

√ **Plan beyond just the EMI.** Factor in maintenance, property taxes, and future expenses.

√ **Your first home doesn't need to be your dream home.** It just needs to be a smart investment.

√ **Stop waiting for the market to crash.** Real estate values historically appreciate over time.

Mini Checklist: Are You Ready to Buy a Home?

- Do you have a stable income?
- Do you have savings for a down payment?
- Do you understand home loans and repayment terms?
- Are you ready to invest in real estate instead of paying rent?
- Do you know the right locations to buy in?

Your Move

If you're still thinking about whether to buy or rent—**ask yourself this:**

√ Would you rather keep paying **someone else's EMI?**

√ Or would you rather invest **in your own future?**

Owning a home is about more than just four walls. **It's financial security, it's stability, and it's a move that sets you up for long-term success.**

Start making smart moves today. **Your future self will thank you.**

Chapter - 2

MONEY MATTERS: HOW TO AFFORD A HOME WITHOUT MAKING COSTLY MISTAKES

So, You Want to Buy a Home, But Can You Afford It?

You've done the math. You've checked your bank balance. And now you're wondering if you should just move into a cave and live off the land.

Because let's be real—**home prices can feel intimidating.**

But here's the bigger picture:

Paying someone else's EMI for the next 20 years and owning nothing is way more expensive.

"The real cost of a home isn't just what's on the
price tag. It's what you're losing by waiting."
— Sashikant & Mairaj

Think about it:

What if your boss gave you two salary options?

√ One where you get paid, but at the end of the year, you have nothing to show for it.

√ One where a portion of your salary goes into an investment that grows over time.

Which one would you choose?

That's the difference between renting and buying. **Renting keeps you stuck in survival mode. Buying builds your future.**

Stop Asking "Can I Afford It?" and Start Asking "How Can I Afford It?"

Most people see a home's price and immediately think, **"No way. That's way out of my league."**

What they **should** be asking is:

"How do I make this happen?"

Because the truth is—you don't need to be a millionaire to own a home. You just need to understand how **money actually works.**

Home Buying Myths vs. Reality

Myth: "You need to pay for a home in full."

Reality: Most homes are bought with home loans, not cash.

Myth: "You need a 20% down payment."

Reality: Many banks offer home loans with as little as 10% down.

Myth: "Buying a home means being broke forever."

Reality: Real estate is one of the best long-term investments you can make.

Myth: "I should wait until I'm financially 'ready'."

Reality: Property prices historically appreciate. The longer you wait, the more expensive it gets.

The True Cost of Homeownership (Beyond Just EMIs, But Don't Panic!)

When most people think about buying a home, they only focus on their **monthly EMI**.

But smart home buyers plan for the full picture:

Down Payment: Typically 10-20% of the home's price. The more you pay upfront, the smaller your EMI.

Registration & Stamp Duty: Varies by state, usually 5-7% of the home price. It's a government charge, so budget for it.

Maintenance & Society Charges: Apartment complexes charge for upkeep — ₹2-₹5 per sq. ft. per month. Higher for gated communities with premium amenities.

Home Loan Interest: Your EMI isn't just repaying the loan—you're also paying the bank's interest. The lower your interest rate, the less you pay in the long run.

Furniture & Interiors: Most homes don't come move-in ready. You'll need essentials like wardrobes, kitchen cabinets, and appliances—another ₹5-10 lakh.

Smart move: Factor these into your budget from day one.

Fix Your Finances Like a Pro

You don't need to be a financial expert to get your money in order. Here's what smart home buyers do:

1. **Clean Up Your Credit Score (Because Banks Reward Financial Discipline)**

   Your **CIBIL score** is basically your financial report card. The higher your score, the better your loan offers.

   - Pay off credit card bills on time.

   - Don't max out your cards (stay below 30% of your credit limit).

   - Avoid multiple loan applications within a short period.

   A 750+ CIBIL score can mean the difference between a ₹ 10,000 EMI and a ₹ 12,000 EMI.

   Over 20 years, that's an extra ₹ **4.8 lakh** paid in interest—just because of a lower score!

2. **Get Serious About Savings (No, Really.)**

   You don't need to survive on instant noodles for six months to save for a home. But you do need a plan.

   Where to Find Extra Money for Your Down Payment:

   - **Cut Unnecessary Expenses:** Pause luxury subscriptions and impulse spending.

   - **Redirect Your Rent:** If you're paying ₹ 30K/month, start treating that as your "home fund."

   - **Use Bonuses Wisely:** That annual bonus? Instead of spending it on vacations, invest it in your future home.

Common Mistakes to Avoid

- Ignoring hidden costs and assuming **only EMI matters.**
- Not checking your **credit score** before applying for a loan.
- Waiting too long and watching **home prices skyrocket.**
- Taking on **too much debt** just because the bank approved it.
- Skipping financial planning and assuming **"it'll work out."**

And here's a costly mistake: Over-leveraging yourself just to buy a bigger house.

If you **stretch your finances too thin**, you'll end up "house poor"—owning a home but struggling to afford anything else. **Plan wisely.**

Mini Checklist: Financial Readiness Before Home Buying

√ Do you have a **stable income** with job security?

√ Is your **credit score 750+** or higher?

√ Do you have enough savings for a **down payment & closing costs?**

√ Have you factored in **maintenance, registration, and other costs?**

√ Are you prepared to **commit to homeownership long-term?**

Your Smartest Move? Get Expert Guidance.

Want expert advice & exclusive home-buying tips?

Scan the QR code below to join our **home buyers' community** and get insider knowledge, property alerts, and guidance from real estate experts.

Chapter - 3

THE DOWN PAYMENT DILEMMA: WHAT'S SMART & WHAT'S STRATEGIC

How Much Do You Really Need To Buy A Home?

One of the biggest myths in home buying is that you **must** save 20% of the home's price before you can even think about purchasing.

That's outdated thinking.

Reality check: Most first-time buyers put down **10-15%**—some even as low as **5%**.

So, why do people still believe in the **20% rule**?

"If you keep waiting to save 20%, you'll end up paying more for the same house in 5 years. Home prices go up. Your salary? Not as fast."
— Sashikant & Mairaj

The Cost Of Waiting (It's Bigger Than You Think)

Fact: The longer you wait, the more expensive real estate gets.

√ **Home prices in India have increased by 8.2% per year over the last decade. (Source: RBI, 2023)**

√ **If you wait 3 years to save an extra ₹ 5L, the home price might go up by ₹ 10L.**

√ **Your EMI could increase because you're now buying at a higher price.**

Bottom line? Saving **too long** can cost you **more** than buying **sooner** with a lower down payment.

Where To Find Your Down Payment (Without Feeling Broke)

Smart buyers don't just "save"—they **strategically** source their down payment from different places:

√ **EPF Withdrawal:** Your Employee Provident Fund can be used for home buying.

√ **Fixed Deposits:** If they're earning less than 6% interest, you're better off using them for your home.

√ **Stocks & Mutual Funds:** Liquidate long-term profits (not emergency funds).

Loan-Friendly Hacks

√ **Builder Discounts:** Some developers offer "low down payment" schemes—just check the fine print.

√ **Co-Borrowing with Family:** Parents or siblings can help improve loan eligibility.

Did you know? Most banks **approve loans with just 10-15% down**. Always ask about **customized loan structures**.

"No Down Payment" Schemes — Are They Right For You?

You've seen the ads:

"Buy A Home With Zero Down Payment!"

Sounds great, right? And for many buyers, it can be a game-changer—**if you pick the right one.**

Here's why it works:

√ **More Buying Power:** No need for a huge upfront sum—you can own a home sooner.

√ **Easier Entry:** A great option for buyers with a steady income but no lump sum saved.

√ **Builder-Backed Benefits:** Some developers offer flexible financing to make homeownership accessible.

But here's what to check first:

- **Interest Rates:** Some loans have higher rates to compensate for the lower down payment. Compare before deciding.
- **Hidden Charges:** Some banks add extra fees. Always read the fine print.

- **Loan Tenure:** A smaller down payment may mean a longer tenure—but you can manage this with **early prepayments.**

"The right No Down Payment scheme makes homeownership possible without financial strain. The wrong one? It costs more in the long run. Always ask the right questions."
— Sashikant & Mairaj

The 3 Golden Rules Of Down Payments

Rule #1: Put down at least 10% if you can. This keeps EMIs reasonable while still getting you into homeownership.

Rule #2: Never drain all your savings for a down payment. You still need an **emergency fund** after you move in.

Rule #3: If you can't afford 10%, reconsider the price range. It's smarter to buy **within your means** than to stretch too thin.

Bonus Tip: If your only option is **5% down**, make **aggressive prepayments** in the first **5 years** to reduce your overall interest.

Common Mistakes To Avoid

- **Waiting too long** to hit 20%, while property prices keep rising.

- **Draining all savings** just to make a bigger down payment.
- **Ignoring builder discounts** or special financing options.

Mini Checklist: Preparing For Your Down Payment

√ Have you explored **EPF withdrawals** or **special offers**?

√ Do you have **at least 3-6 months of emergency savings** after the down payment?

√ Have you checked **loan options** that allow flexible down payments?

Ready To Buy? Get Expert Help!

Scan the QR code below to join our **exclusive buyer community** for expert advice and real-world home-buying tips.

Chapter - 4

DEVELOPERS & BROKERS: WHO'S ACTUALLY ON YOUR SIDE?

Who's Who In Real Estate?

When buying a home, you'll likely interact with **two key players—brokers** and **developers**. Each plays an important role, and understanding how they work will help you navigate the process with confidence.

Brokers: The Middlemen Who Match Buyers & Properties

A broker's job is to **connect buyers and sellers**. Some brokers genuinely work to find buyers the right home, while others focus primarily on closing deals quickly.

What a good broker does:

√ Helps you find properties that match your needs.

√ Guides you through negotiations and paperwork.

√ Provides insights about market trends and pricing.

What you should check before choosing a broker:

√ Are they showing you multiple options or just one project they're prioritizing?

√ Are they transparent about any **builder tie-ups** or commissions they receive?

√ Are they rushing you into a decision instead of allowing you time to evaluate?

Pro Tip: A good broker provides options, **not pressure**. If you feel rushed, step back and re-evaluate.

Developers: More Than Just Sellers — They Shape Communities

Developers **do more than sell homes—they build communities, enhance cities, and create spaces for families to grow**.

A **reliable developer** focuses on **quality, transparency, and long-term value**.

What a trustworthy developer does:

√ Delivers projects **on time** with **clear commitments.**

√ Uses **high-quality materials** and maintains construction standards.

√ Offers **transparent pricing** with **well-defined agreements.**

What you should check before booking a property:

√ **RERA Registration** – Ensures regulatory compliance and buyer protection.

√ **Past Projects** – Visit completed projects to check quality and maintenance.

√ **What's Delivered vs. Brochures** – Show flats give an idea, but **always ask what's included in writing.**

Pro Tip: Pre-launch offers can be excellent opportunities, but always **verify approvals before committing**.

Brokers: Do You Really Need One?

Brokers can be **helpful**, but they're not **always necessary**.

When a broker can add value:

√ If you're buying from an **individual seller** and need help with **negotiation.**

√ If you're looking for **resale properties** that aren't widely listed.

When you can buy without a broker:

√ If you're buying **directly from a reputed developer.**

√ If you have access to **verified listings** and can negotiate independently.

Pro Tip: A great home doesn't need aggressive selling. If a property is truly valuable, it will speak for itself.

Developers: How To Choose The Right One

The **developer you choose** determines the **quality** and **security** of your investment.

What to look for before selecting a developer:

√ **RERA Registration** – Ensures **legal approvals** and protects buyers.

√ **Past Projects** – Visit previous developments and talk to residents.

√ **Timely Possession** – Check whether past projects were delivered **on time.**

Pro Tip: A **strong track record speaks louder than marketing**. A good developer's **reputation is built on past success.**

What To Verify Before Signing Any Agreement

√ 3D Walkthroughs & Show Flats – Ask for a **detailed list** of what's actually included.

√ **Amenities & Facilities** – Ensure everything promised will be **delivered and maintained.**

√ **Legal Approvals** – Confirm the project's **RERA registration** and legal status.

Pro Tip: The **best developers build trust, not just homes.**

Common Mistakes To Avoid

- Relying on **a broker without verifying their credentials.**
- Ignoring **RERA compliance and legal approvals.**
- Skipping a **visit to past projects** to check real quality.
- Trusting **verbal commitments** instead of written agreements.

Mini Checklist: Finding The Right Real Estate Partner

√ Have you **verified your broker's track record** and previous client feedback?

√ Have you checked if your broker is offering **exclusive properties** or just **common listings**?

√ Have you visited **the builder's past projects** to compare **promises vs. reality?**

√ Have you confirmed **RERA compliance** before committing?

Get Expert Guidance – Join Our Community

Scan the QR code below to join our **exclusive home buyer community** for expert guidance, real-world insights, and the best home-buying tips.

Chapter - 5

HOW TO SPOT THE RIGHT PROPERTY (WITHOUT WASTING EVERY WEEKEND)

"Location, Location, Location" – But What Does That Actually Mean?

Buying a home isn't just about the **size of the rooms** or the **aesthetic appeal**. A great home should fit seamlessly into your **lifestyle, finances, and long-term goals**.

Many buyers fall in love with a **stunning living room** or a **breathtaking balcony view**—only to realize later that their dream home comes with **daily traffic jams, high maintenance costs, or limited resale value**.

A **smart home-buying decision** isn't based on just what looks good today—it's about choosing a property that enhances your **quality of life** and **financial security** for years to come.

The Non-Negotiables: What Your Future Home MUST Have

Beyond brochures and glossy marketing, these are the **critical factors** you should prioritize:

1. **Location (It's More Than Just a "Good Area")**

   - **Commute Check** – Will getting to work or school be a daily struggle? A **shorter commute** can literally **add years to your life**.

   - **Noise Levels** – Visit at different times of the day. What seems peaceful at noon might be **too noisy** at night.

   - **Future Growth** – Are **metros, IT hubs, or business districts** being developed nearby? Areas with **strong infrastructure growth** tend to **appreciate in value faster**.

   - **Essential Amenities** – Are **hospitals, schools, grocery stores, and daily conveniences** within easy reach?

   Pro Tip: A **dream home** in the **wrong location** can turn into a **daily hassle**. Think **beyond today**—where will this area be in **5-10 years**?

Hidden Red Flags That Can Ruin Your Investment

Some property issues **aren't obvious** at first glance. These are **common but often ignored:**

1. **Structural Quality & Construction Materials**

   - **Check Wall Strength** – Tap on walls; do they sound hollow? **Lighter materials** like AAC blocks are common but can feel less sturdy.

   - **Mivan Formwork Walls** – Some modern projects use **high-quality reinforced concrete walls** for **durability and fewer cracks**.

- **Water Stains & Uneven Paint** – These may indicate **leakage issues** or **rushed construction**.

2. **Water Supply & Drainage**

    - **Turn on All Taps** – Weak water pressure could indicate a **plumbing problem**.

    - **Flush Toilets** – Slow drainage could mean a **blocked or faulty pipeline**.

    - **Check for Water Tanker Dependence** – If a project **doesn't have a dedicated water source, monthly maintenance costs** can be **higher**.

3. **Legal Documentation & Approvals**

    - **RERA Registration** – A **RERA-registered** project ensures compliance with government regulations.

    - **Encumbrance Certificate** – Confirms the property is **free of legal disputes**.

    - **Project Approvals** – Always verify that the **land title, building permissions, and environmental clearances** are **in place**.

    Pro Tip: Even reputed developers can experience **approval delays**. Always **verify the paperwork** before committing.

Negotiation: How to Get a Solid Deal Without Overpaying

A **home purchase** is part **research**, part **negotiation**. The **best deals** go to those who **ask the right questions** and **stay informed**.

3 Smart Buyer Negotiation Strategies:

√ **Don't Show Excitement Too Soon** – If you say "I LOVE this place!" too early, you lose your **bargaining power**. Stay **neutral**.

√ **Know the Market Rate** – Compare **similar properties in the area** before making an offer. If a **price seems inflated**, you **have room to negotiate**.

√ **Leverage Payment Flexibility** – Many developers offer **customized payment plans**. Ask about options that fit your **financial situation**.

Pro Tip: Every price is negotiable. Developers **expect** some negotiation, so don't accept the first offer blindly.

Common Mistakes to Avoid

- **Falling for beautifully staged show apartments** without checking the **actual unit's construction quality**.

- **Ignoring maintenance costs**—a home isn't just about the price tag; **running costs matter**.

- **Skipping legal verification** assuming everything is fine just because **"others are buying it"**.

- **Not considering resale value**—what happens when you want to **sell the home later?**

Mini Checklist: Are You Choosing the Right Property?

- Have you verified the **location's future growth potential?**

- Did you **visit at different times of the day** to check for **noise and livability?**

- Is the project **RERA-registered and legally approved**?
- Have you checked **water supply, drainage, and maintenance costs**?
- Did you compare **market prices** before finalizing your deal?

Join Our Exclusive Home Buyer's Community

Scan the QR code below to connect with **experts**, get **insider insights**, and make the **smartest** home-buying decision.

Chapter - 6

THE HOME INSPECTION SURVIVAL GUIDE

The Truth About Home Inspections (And Why They Matter)

Buying a home is one of the biggest financial decisions you'll ever make. And while it's easy to get excited about **moving in**, the smart buyer knows that **a final inspection is non-negotiable**.

Why? Because even the **best homes**—whether newly constructed or resale—can have minor **finishing issues**. A proper home inspection ensures that you're not **stuck with unexpected repairs** after moving in.

A **well-built home** should be **safe, structurally sound, and hassle-free**. This chapter will help you **check for key details** so that your home is everything you expect it to be—before you sign on the dotted line.

Home Inspection Myths (Don't Fall for Them)

√ **"It's a new building—nothing to check."** Even **brand-new homes** can have **minor finishing defects**—paintwork, fittings, or last-minute fixes before handover. **A quick check helps flag anything that needs attention upfront.**

√ **"I'll just do a quick walkthrough."** A proper home inspection means checking essentials—**plumbing, wiring, ventilation, drainage, and fittings**. Spending an extra hour now can save **lakhs in long-term costs**.

The Smart Buyer's Home Inspection Checklist

1. **Structural Quality & Materials**

   - **Walls & Floors** – Tap on walls. Hollow sounds? Some walls use **lightweight AAC blocks**, which are standard but may offer **less sound insulation**.

   - **Mivan Formwork Walls** – These are **strong, crack-resistant, and durable**. Just ensure the finishing is smooth and there are no signs of **moisture seepage**.

   - **Doors & Windows** – Open and close them. **Misalignment** might just be a minor adjustment. But if multiple doors don't shut properly, **flag it for a fix**.

   - **Floor Leveling** – Drop a marble on the floor. If it rolls in one direction, the **flooring might be uneven**—something to check with the builder.

2. **Water Supply & Plumbing**

   - **Turn on All Taps** – Low water pressure? This could be temporary, but it's worth checking with the society.

   - **Flush the Toilets** – Slow drainage could mean **pipeline issues**—ask for confirmation.

   - **Check for Leakage Signs** – Water stains near ceilings or corners can indicate **waterproofing problems**.

- **Tankers vs. Municipal Water** – Some buildings depend on water tankers. If so, **check how frequently they are needed** and how this affects **monthly costs**.

3. **Electrical & Wiring**
   - **Power Sockets** – Plug in a charger. If it sparks or feels loose, it might need **immediate attention**.
   - **Switchboard Quality** – Press multiple switches—do lights flicker? That could mean **loose wiring**.
   - **Backup Power** – Does the society have **generator backup**? If yes, check which areas it covers—**lifts, common areas, or individual flats**.
   - **Main Circuit Breaker (MCB)** – Flip the switch to test if it actually **cuts off power as expected**.

4. **Natural Light & Ventilation**
   - Spend **30 minutes inside the home at different times of the day**—does it feel **airy or stuffy**?
   - Does the flat get enough **natural sunlight**?
   - Good ventilation reduces electricity bills and **prevents moisture buildup**.
   - **Check phone signal strength**—Some high-rises have poor network coverage.

5. **Common Area & Parking Check**
   - **Visit the parking area at night**—Is it **well-lit and secure**?
   - **Check the elevators**—Are they **slow or shaky**? Test them **at peak hours**.
   - **Walk around the society**—Are common areas **well-maintained**? A **clean, well-kept society** signals good **long-term upkeep**.

The "Live Test" – Experience the Home Before You Buy

Seeing a property **once in daylight isn't enough**. Try this:

- **Visit at different times** – A quiet morning neighborhood might be a high-traffic zone in the evening.

- **Stand on the balcony** – Are you breathing **fresh air or dust from a nearby construction site?**

- **Feel the temperature** – Some flats get **too hot or too cold** due to ventilation or insulation quality.

- **Check your mobile network – You don't want a home where you have to stand near the window to make a call.**

Pro Tip: Some issues only show up **after you move in**. That's why many buyers recommend visiting the property **twice before finalizing**.

Common Mistakes to Avoid

- **Skipping the inspection because it's a new property.** Even great developers **expect buyers to do a quality check before handover.**

- **Checking the home only in one season or one time of day.** Conditions change.

- **Relying only on online photos.** The camera hides more than it reveals.

- **Ignoring minor red flags**. Fixing them later costs more than catching them now.

Mini Checklist: Home Inspection Essentials

√ No **major structural cracks** or **misaligned doors/windows**

√ Water pressure is **strong**, no **leakage stains**

√ All **electrical fittings** are functional, **no sparking sockets**

√ **Good ventilation, sunlight, and fresh airflow**

√ **Safe, well-maintained common areas & parking**

Pro Tip: The best developers appreciate when buyers do their own quality checks. It ensures both parties are on the same page before possession.

Your Final Step: Get Ready to Own with Confidence

A home that **looks great** but has **hidden issues** is like a shiny new car with a **faulty engine.**

A little extra effort before buying can **save you years of frustration** and help you move into a home you **truly love.**

Want expert guidance on home buying?

Scan the QR code to join our buyer's community for **insider tips & expert insights.**

SECTION 2

FINANCING & CLOSING
LIKE A PRO

Your Bank Wants to Make Money Off You. Let's Flip the Script.

Home loans are designed to make **the bank rich**. Not you.

Think about it—**banks will happily lend you money** while smiling at you, but behind the scenes? They're calculating exactly **how much they can earn from you** over the next 15-30 years.

And if you don't know what you're doing?

√ You **end up paying lakhs extra** in interest just because you picked the **wrong loan type.**

√ You assume **the EMI is all you have to worry about**—then get **slapped with hidden fees** that weren't on the glossy brochure.

√ You blindly **trust the bank's advice,** forgetting that their goal **isn't to help you**—it's to maximize their profit.

But not you. Not anymore.

In this section, we're going to **turn the tables** so that **you win at the home loan game** instead of being trapped by it.

What You'll Learn:

√ The real difference between **fixed and floating rates** (and which one actually benefits YOU).

√ The **secret negotiation tricks** that banks don't want you to know **(yes, you can negotiate your loan).**

√ The **hidden costs of home loans** that wreck most buyers—processing fees, prepayment penalties, and more.

√ How to **set up your finances smartly** so you don't end up **drowning in debt.**

A **home loan isn't just an EMI.** It's a **long-term financial strategy.** If you **plan it right,** you'll **build wealth while paying off your home.** If you **don't,** you'll **overpay by lakhs.**

Read this. Master this. Or get ready to **donate a fortune to the bank.**

Chapter - 7

MORTGAGES 101 – UNDERSTANDING HOME LOANS WITHOUT A FINANCE DEGREE

Why Understanding Home Loans is Non-Negotiable

Most people spend **more time researching their next phone** than they do their home loan. That's a financial disaster waiting to happen.

A **home loan isn't just an EMI**—it's a long-term financial strategy. **Play it smart, and you're building wealth**. Play it wrong, and you're stuck in **avoidable debt for decades**.

What most buyers don't realize:

√ **Banks love home loans** — not because they're generous, but because they make a fortune from them.

√ **A 30-year loan can mean paying nearly double** the original home price in interest.

√ **That ₹ 1 crore apartment?** After 30 years, you might have paid ₹ 1.9 crore in total.

So before you sign anything, let's **break it down—without the boring finance jargon**.

36

Types of Home Loans:
Which One is Right for You?

1. **Fixed vs. Floating Interest Rates – What Works Best?**
   - **Fixed Rate Loan**
   - EMI stays **the same** throughout the tenure.
   - No surprises—**predictable payments** make budgeting easier.
   - Typically **higher interest rates** than floating loans.
   - **Floating Rate Loan**
   - Interest rate **fluctuates** based on market conditions.
   - **Lower rates** when markets dip.
   - **Riskier** — EMIs can rise if rates increase.

   Pro Tip: Some banks offer a **semi-fixed rate**—fixed for the first 5-10 years, then switches to floating. This offers stability upfront with flexibility later.

   What to Check: If you go with **floating rates**, confirm whether you can switch to **fixed rates later without high conversion fees.**

2. **Loan Tenure – How Long Should You Stretch It?**

   A **shorter tenure** = Higher EMIs, **but less total interest paid**.

   A **longer tenure** = Lower EMIs, **but you pay more in interest over time.**

   Example:
   - A ₹ 50 lakh loan at 8% interest for 15 years → ₹ 86 lakh total repayment.
   - The same loan for 30 years → ₹ 1.32 crore total repayment.

- That's ₹ 46 lakh extra interest just for choosing a longer tenure.

Smart Hack: If you need a **longer tenure for manageable EMIs**, start **prepaying small amounts early**. Even ₹ **5,000 extra per month** can cut years off your loan.

3. **The Down Payment Strategy: How Much Do You REALLY Need?**

- **Standard down payment** = 20% of the property price.
- Some banks allow **10% down, but lower down payments = higher total interest paid.**

Real Stat: Homebuyers who put **20% or more down save an average of 15% in interest payments** over their loan tenure. *(Source: Economic Times)*

Pro Tip: The longer you wait to save a big down payment, the more home prices increase. If waiting another 3 years to save ₹ 5 lakh means the home price rises by ₹ 10 lakh, **you're losing money.**

How Banks Approve (or Reject) Your Loan

Think banks just hand out loans to anyone? Think again. Here's what they **actually** check:

1. **Your CIBIL Score – Why It Matters More Than You Think**

   Your CIBIL score determines:

   - **Your loan eligibility** — higher scores = better approval chances.
   - **Your interest rate** — a higher score gets you lower rates.
   - **Loan amount**—a lower score may mean **lower approved limits**.

- **750+ Score = Best rates, fastest approvals**.
- **Below 700?** Higher interest, lower loan amount, possible rejection.

Pro Tip: Even a 0.5% lower interest rate can save you lakhs over your loan tenure.

Example:

√ A ₹ 75 lakh loan at **8.5% vs. 8.0%** might seem like a small difference.

√ **But** over 20 years, that's an extra `**6-8 lakh in interest paid.**

How to improve your **CIBIL score before applying**:

√ Pay off **credit card** bills on time.

√ Don't **max out** your credit card limit.

√ Avoid applying for **multiple loans at once.**

The Hidden Costs of Home Loans That Can Wreck You

1. **Processing Fees – The Silent Killer**

   - Banks charge **0.5% to 1% of the loan amount** just for approving your loan.

   - Some banks **refund it if the loan is rejected.** Others don't—**always ask.**

2. **Prepayment Penalties – When Paying Early Costs You**

   - **Some banks charge a penalty** if you try to **pay off your loan early**.

   - Check the **prepayment rules before signing** anything.

3. **Insurance Banks "Highly Recommend" (a.k.a. Push on You)**

- **Banks often bundle loan insurance**—sometimes useful, but **not always necessary**.
- Some **increase your EMI slightly** to cover it.
- Always read the fine print. **Know if you need it or not.**

Common Mistakes to Avoid

- **Assuming EMI is the only cost**—ignoring hidden charges.
- **Not checking your CIBIL score** before applying.
- **Choosing the longest tenure possible** just for lower EMIs—paying way more in interest.
- **Taking the first loan offer** without comparing options.
- **Skipping the fine print**—processing fees, prepayment charges, foreclosure rules.

Mini Checklist: Understanding Your Mortgage

√ Do you know the **difference between fixed-rate and floating-rate loans**?

√ Have you **compared loan offers** from multiple banks?

√ Have you **checked your CIBIL score** and improved it before applying?

√ Do you know **the total interest** amount you'll pay over your loan tenure?

√ Have you calculated **how much EMI you can comfortably afford**?

√ Have you checked for **hidden charges** like processing fees and penalties?

√ Do you know your **bank's foreclosure policy**—can you **pay off early** without penalties?

Final Thoughts: Your Loan, Your Terms

A **home loan is more than just an EMI.** It's a **tool to build wealth**—but only if you use it wisely.

√ **Negotiate interest rates.**

√ **Read the fine print** on hidden charges.

√ **Choose tenure wisely**—don't overextend just for lower EMIs.

√ **Prepay when you can**—the faster you close the loan, the less interest you pay.

Don't let the bank be the only winner in your home-buying journey. Be **smart, strategic, and financially prepared.**

Join Our Exclusive Home Buyers' Community!

Scan the QR code below to get expert insights, home-buying tips, and loan negotiation hacks from industry pros.

A **home loan is more than just an EMI.** It's a **tool to build wealth**—but only if you use it wisely.

Chapter - 8

EMI & HOMEOWNERSHIP: PLANNING SMART, LIVING STRESS-FREE

Your EMI is Just One Part of Homeownership Here's How to Plan Wisely

Buying a home is one of the most empowering financial moves you can make. Instead of paying rent with nothing to show for it, you're building equity, securing your future, and creating a space that's truly yours.

But smart homeownership isn't just about getting a good deal—it's about understanding **the full picture** so that you can enjoy your home stress-free.

By planning for **all aspects** of homeownership—beyond just the EMI—you'll set yourself up for a **smooth, predictable, and financially secure journey.**

Beyond the EMI: What Every Smart Buyer Should Consider

Most people focus only on **how much their EMI will be**— but that's just one part of the equation. Think of homeownership as a well-planned investment where, along with your EMI, a few other factors come into play.

These aren't "extra costs" to worry about—they're just **part of the homeownership experience**. And the best part? With a little planning, they're easy to manage.

Let's break it down.

What to Factor in (and How to Stay in Control)

1. Society Maintenance – The Cost of Comfortable Living

When you live in a **well-maintained gated community**, you're not just paying for four walls—you're getting **security, cleanliness, and modern amenities** like landscaped gardens, elevators, clubhouses, and gyms.

√ **What to Expect:**

- Maintenance fees range from **₹2–₹5 per sq. ft. per month**, depending on amenities.

- Premium societies with **pools, gyms, and smart security systems** may have slightly higher costs—but they also **enhance property value** over time.

√ **How to Stay in Control:**

- **Ask for a fee breakdown** before buying so there are no surprises.

- **Check how often fees increase**—a small, steady rise is normal for upkeep.

- **Look for a well-managed society**—a well-run complex can keep costs stable while maintaining quality.

2. Property Tax – Your Contribution to City Development

Every homeowner contributes property tax, which goes toward **city infrastructure, roads, and public services**. It's a small price to pay for better surroundings and future growth.

√ **What to Expect:**

- Varies based on **location, property size, and municipal rates**.

- Major metro cities may see **small annual increases** as areas develop and improve.

√ **How to Stay in Control:**

- **Know the current property tax slab**—it's usually straightforward and predictable.

- **Factor this into your budget**—it's typically a fraction of your EMI.

- **Consider it an investment**—well-developed areas see better resale values.

3. Stamp Duty & Registration – The Final Step to Ownership

This is the **one-time official process** that legally makes the home yours. Builders and banks can guide you through it, and it's **fully transparent and predictable**.

√ **What to Expect:**

- **Stamp duty & registration fees** range from **7-10% of the property value**, depending on state laws.

- Many builders offer **assistance or payment plans** to help ease this process.

√ **How to Stay in Control:**

- **Confirm the exact costs upfront**—no surprises.
- **Plan for this in your home budget**—it's a **one-time step** that ensures a smooth purchase.
- **Check for government incentives**—some states offer rebates for first-time buyers.

4. Home Upgrades & Personalization – Making It Yours

Moving into a **brand-new home** is exciting, and many buyers like to **personalize their space**. Whether it's adding modular kitchen fittings, extra wardrobes, or designer lighting, these little touches make your house feel like home.

√ **What to Expect:**

- Basic fittings are always included, but some buyers may want **custom interiors**.
- Typical move-in upgrades range from **₹50,000 to ₹2 lakh**, depending on preferences.

√ **How to Stay in Control:**

- **Prioritize essentials first**—furniture, storage, and lighting.
- **Upgrade in stages**—there's no rush to do everything at once.
- **Opt for builder customization offers**—some developers offer ready-made interior packages.

Building Your Homeowner's Safety Net

Owning a home is a **stable, long-term financial move,** and just like with any major investment, it's good to have a safety cushion.

A little financial planning **before you buy** means you'll never have to worry later.

√ **The Smart Safety Net Plan:**

- **Set aside 3-6 months' worth of EMIs**—it's always good to have a buffer.

- **Plan for annual property costs** (tax, maintenance) so they never feel unexpected.

- **Budget a small amount for improvements**—your home will grow with you over time.

With these in place, you can enjoy homeownership **stress-free, knowing you're covered for anything.**

Common Mistakes to Avoid

- **Thinking the EMI is the only cost**—just like rent, there are always small additional factors.

- **Not asking about society maintenance fees upfront**—it's always best to check in advance.

- **Skipping a financial buffer**—having a small safety net makes life easier.

- **Assuming homeownership is complicated**—in reality, with a little planning, it's seamless.

Mini Checklist: Smart Homeownership Planning

√ Do you know the estimated maintenance costs for your society?

√ Have you factored in property tax for your area?

√ Do you have a plan for registration & stamp duty costs?

√ Are you budgeting for personal upgrades at your own pace?

√ Have you set aside a simple safety net for peace of mind?

Final Thought: A Home is an Investment in Your Future

Buying a home isn't just about having a place to live—it's about **stability, security, and financial growth.**

√ **Plan smart**—a little preparation makes homeownership seamless.

√ **Think long-term**—a home appreciates in value, making it a powerful asset.

√ **Enjoy the journey**—this is your space, your future, your investment.

With the right mindset and a simple plan, homeownership is not just achievable—it's one of the best financial decisions you'll ever make.

Join Our Exclusive Home Buyer's Community!

Want expert insights, home-buying tips, and practical strategies?

Scan the QR code below to connect with **seasoned homebuyers, real estate experts, and financial planners**—and make your home-buying journey effortless.

Chapter - 9

MAKING AN OFFER THAT SAVES YOU LAKHS — THE SMART WAY

A Good Offer Isn't About Bargaining — It's About Strategy

Buying a home is a life-changing investment. You're not just purchasing four walls—you're securing your future, building wealth, and creating a space that's truly yours.

While property prices are often set based on market conditions, many homebuyers don't realize that they have room to **customize their deal**—not just in pricing, but in payment plans, amenities, and added benefits.

The smartest buyers aren't those who haggle endlessly, but those who **know when to ask, what to ask for, and how to make their purchase work in their favor.**

Why a Thoughtful Approach Saves You Lakhs

Most people assume that the listed price is the final price. But here's the reality:

√ **Builders offer structured pricing** based on market trends, construction timelines, and available inventory.

√ **Resale sellers set prices higher** than what they expect, anticipating some negotiation.

√ **Exclusive buyer incentives**—like payment flexibility, added features, or better financing terms—are often available if you ask the right way.

A successful negotiation isn't about lowballing—it's about **structuring your offer smartly** so both you and the developer win.

How to Make a Smart Offer (That Developers Respect & Accept Faster)

1. Do Your Research Before Discussing Price

- Check the **market rate** of similar homes in the area.

- Ask the developer about **any ongoing promotions or offers**.

- Compare different units within the project sometimes, a slightly different layout offers better value.

Pro Tip: If you're serious about a property, let the developer know. A genuine buyer often gets priority when final pricing is discussed.

2. Show Interest, But Stay Strategic

- Avoid saying, "This is my dream home!" too soon.

- Instead, express interest while keeping it professional: "I like this property, and I'm considering it along with another option. I'd love to understand if there are any current promotions."

Why This Works: Developers appreciate **informed buyers** who value quality and are open to discussing structured deals rather than just price drops.

3. Ask About Payment Flexibility Instead of Just Discounts

- Developers often provide **customized payment plans** to make home-buying easier.

- Instead of just asking for a price reduction, ask: "Do you have any flexible payment schemes or lower upfront costs?"

- This helps you manage cash flow better **without affecting the developer's project plan.**

Why This Works: Developers prefer structured payments over sudden price drops. A flexible plan can be a win-win for both.

4. Consider Pre-Launch Offers & Exclusive Deals

- Many buyers wait until a project is fully ready—but early buyers often get the best value.

- **Pre-launch pricing** is designed to reward early buyers, and developers may offer:

- Better unit selection.

- Additional interior upgrades.

- More payment flexibility.

Pro Tip: If the project is under RERA, all approvals are in place. If you're considering a pre-launch, **always verify registration details** for extra confidence.

5. Smart Extras: What You Can Ask For

Instead of focusing only on price, **look at the bigger picture.** Ask about:

- **Parking inclusion** (worth ₹3-5 lakh in many projects).

- **Fixed maintenance charges** for the first 2-3 years.

- **Early possession benefits** (sometimes available if your unit is ready sooner).

Why This Works: Developers can often accommodate **value-add requests** instead of just adjusting the price.

Hidden Costs You Should Factor Into Your Offer

1. **Stamp Duty, GST & Registration**
   - Stamp duty & registration typically **adds 7-10%** to the cost.
   - Under-construction homes may include **GST (5-12%)**.
   - Some developers **offer all-inclusive pricing**—always ask for clarity.

2. **Maintenance & Society Fees**
   - Confirm the **monthly maintenance cost** and whether it's fixed for the first few years.
   - Ask if **corpus fund contributions** are included in the total cost.

3. **Parking & Additional Amenities**
   - Some societies charge **separately for parking**—always confirm what's included.
   - Clubhouse memberships or other premium services **may have one-time fees.**

Mini Checklist: Making the Right Offer

√ Have you researched the price of similar properties in the area?

√ Are you asking about **payment flexibility, not just discounts?**

√ Have you checked what's included in the final price (parking, maintenance, etc.)?

√ Did you express genuine interest while still keeping your options open?

√ Are you looking at **total value instead of just the per-square-foot rate?**

Common Mistakes to Avoid

- Focusing only on price without considering the value of developer-backed offers.

- Ignoring pre-launch deals that could offer better financial benefits.

- Relying only on verbal agreements—always get details in writing.

- Not factoring in stamp duty, GST, and other standard charges into the offer.

- Thinking short-term instead of looking at future appreciation potential.

Final Thought: Negotiation Isn't Just About Discounts—It's About Value

The best homebuyers aren't those who get the biggest discount—they're the ones who structure the best deal for **long-term value, payment flexibility, and investment potential.**

A strong offer isn't just about "saving money"—it's about **maximizing what you get for what you pay.**

Join Our Exclusive Home Buyer's Community!

Want insider tips and expert-backed strategies?

Scan the QR code below to connect with **seasoned homebuyers, real estate professionals, and financial advisors—** and make your home-buying journey effortless.

SECTION 3

SEALING THE DEAL & MOVING IN

Your Home is Almost Yours - Let's Finish Strong

You're at the final stretch. The paperwork is done. The loan is approved. You've mentally moved in and already planned where your furniture will go.

But before you celebrate, there are a few crucial last steps.

This is where buyers often **overlook details**, leading to unnecessary stress later. A little extra care now can make your transition into homeownership seamless.

What You'll Learn in This Section:

√ The **final paperwork checks** that ensure your home purchase is legally sound.

√ The **final walkthrough checklist**—ensuring your home is delivered exactly as promised.

√ What to do if there are **possession delays**, and how to handle them with confidence.

√ How to **transition smoothly from buyer to homeowner** without stress.

This section is designed to help you **lock in every detail with confidence** so that when you step into your new home, you do so without a single worry.

Let's make sure you **seal the deal like a pro.**

Chapter - 10

THE PAPERWORK MAZE - GETTING IT RIGHT FROM DAY ONE

Why the Right Paperwork Protects Your Home & Peace of Mind

Buying a home is one of the most exciting moments of your life. But beyond the stunning architecture and beautiful interiors, the real foundation of your property is its **paperwork**.

Every professional developer ensures transparency in documentation, making the home-buying journey smooth and worry-free. However, as a buyer, it's your responsibility to **understand every clause and verify the details**—so that you walk into homeownership with complete confidence.

This chapter will help you **decode the legal documents** involved in buying a home, ensuring that everything is in place before you sign.

The Most Important Documents You Need to Check (And Why They Matter)

1. Sale Agreement: The Blueprint of Your Home Purchase

This isn't just a formality—it's the **legal contract** that confirms the terms of your purchase. It covers:

- **Price & Payment Terms** – Make sure all costs are clearly mentioned, including GST, maintenance, parking, and other charges.

- **Possession Date & Commitments** – Reputed developers honor their timelines, but in the rare case of delays, the agreement should clearly outline the next steps.

- **Penalty Clause for Payment Delays** – Developers ensure project timelines by maintaining structured payment schedules. Understanding this clause keeps your purchase stress-free.

Pro Tip: Always read this document carefully. If anything seems unclear, ask the developer's sales team—they're there to help.

2. Title Deed: Proof of Clear Ownership

Your developer will always provide clear title documentation, ensuring the property is legally sound. Still, it's good practice to verify:

- **Ownership History** – Confirm that the land and project belong to the developer with full legal rights.

- **Encumbrance Certificate** – Confirms that the property is free from any mortgage or legal disputes.

- **Land Use Approval** – Ensures that the property is designated for residential use.

Pro Tip: Developers with strong reputations ensure their projects are legally sound. Still, reviewing these documents adds an extra layer of confidence.

3. RERA Registration: Your Assurance of Quality & Transparency

The **Real Estate Regulatory Authority (RERA)** was established to protect homebuyers and ensure smooth project execution. A **RERA-registered project** guarantees:

- **On-time delivery** – Developers commit to structured construction timelines.

- **Full transparency** – Every detail of the project is listed, from approvals to completion status.

- **Buyer Protection** – In case of unexpected delays, RERA guidelines ensure fair solutions for buyers.

How to Check a Project's RERA Status:

Visit your state's **official RERA website.**

Enter the **developer's name or project name.**

Verify the **registration number, approvals, and construction timelines.**

Pro Tip: Choosing a RERA-approved project is one of the smartest decisions a buyer can make.

Hidden Costs? Not If You Plan Smart

A great developer ensures transparency in pricing. However, buyers often overlook a few **standard costs** associated with home buying. Here's what you should factor in:

1. **Stamp Duty & Registration (Government Fees, Not Developer Charges)**

- Typically 7-10% **of the property value,** paid to the government.

- Some developers offer **all-inclusive pricing**—always ask for clarity.

2. Parking & Maintenance Fees

- Parking in premium locations **may have additional costs**—confirm what's included.

- Maintenance fees cover **security, amenities, and upkeep**—some societies charge a one-time corpus fund to ensure long-term maintenance.

3. Home Loan Processing & Bank Charges

- Loan processing fees range from **0.5% to 1%** of the loan amount.

- Banks may require **home loan insurance**—this is optional but recommended for security.

Pro Tip: Always get a **detailed cost breakdown** from your developer to plan your finances better.

Common Buyer Mistakes (And How to Avoid Them)

√ **Skipping document verification.** Always check legal approvals—even the best projects have paperwork that needs review.

√ **Not asking about extra costs upfront.** Get a clear cost breakdown before signing.

√ **Trusting verbal agreements.** Always get commitments in writing for full clarity.

√ **Ignoring the RERA verification step.** It's a simple check that ensures your project is legally sound.

Your Paperwork Checklist Before Signing

√ Have you reviewed the **Sale Agreement** and clarified any questions?

√ Have you checked the **Title Deed** to confirm clear ownership?

√ Have you verified that the project is **RERA-registered**?

√ Have you accounted for **stamp duty, registration, and other standard costs?**

√ Have you received a **cost breakdown in writing** from the developer?

Final Thought: Your Home is an Investment—Protect It from Day One

Buying from a **reputable developer** ensures that your home's legal and financial foundation is strong. **A little due diligence now guarantees stress-free homeownership later.**

Join Our Exclusive Home Buyer's Community!

Scan the QR code below to connect with experts, get insights, and ensure you make the smartest decision for your future home.

[QR Code]

What's Next?

√ Now that your paperwork is in place, let's move to the next big step:

√ **Your Final Walkthrough & Getting the Keys to Your Home.**

Chapter - 11

FINAL WALKTHROUGH & GETTING THE KEYS TO YOUR HOME

Your Home is Ready. Let's Make Sure Everything is Perfect.

You're just one step away from homeownership!

But before you accept the keys, **one final check is crucial.** A final walkthrough ensures that:

√ Your home is **delivered exactly as promised**.

√ All utilities and amenities are functioning properly.

√ Any final touch-ups or minor adjustments are addressed **before** you move in.

This is your moment to verify everything and ensure a **smooth, hassle-free move-in experience.**

The 10-Step Final Walkthrough Checklist

1. Walls, Ceilings & Flooring – Quality Check

- Check for any **cracks, uneven paint, or damp spots**.
- Tap on walls—hollow sounds indicate lighter materials, which is normal in modern construction.

2. **Doors & Windows – Proper Installation**

    - Open and close **all doors and windows**—they should align smoothly.

    - Ensure **locking systems** function correctly.

3. **Electrical Fittings – Power Check**

    - Test **all light switches, fans, and sockets.**

    - Plug in a charger to ensure power flow to every outlet.

    - Check the **main circuit breaker (MCB)** to ensure it properly cuts off power when switched off.

4. **Plumbing & Water Supply – No Leaks Allowed**

    - Turn on **all taps and showers**—water pressure should be strong.

    - Flush all toilets—water should drain properly.

    - Look for any **leakage stains** around pipes.

5. **Drainage & Ventilation – Essential for Comfort**

    - Pour a **bucket of water in bathrooms and balconies**— it should drain properly.

    - Ensure the kitchen has **proper ventilation and exhaust systems.**

6. **Safety & Security Features – Peace of Mind**

    - Check if the **main door lock and security system** work properly.

    - Ask about **CCTV coverage** and security personnel availability.

7. **Utility Connections – Water, Gas & Electricity**

    - Confirm that **water and electricity meters** are installed and functioning.

- Ensure your gas pipeline (if applicable) is **secure and connected.**

8. **Common Areas & Parking – The Full Experience**
   - Visit your **designated parking space** and confirm it matches your agreement.
   - Walk around common areas—check the **elevator, corridors, and society amenities.**

9. **Legal Handover Kit – What You Should Receive**
   - Copy of **all legal documents** (sale deed, possession letter, warranties).
   - Contact details for **maintenance staff and society management.**
   - User manuals for **electrical appliances, elevators, and generators** (if applicable).

10. **Document Any Issues – Fix Before You Move In**
    - If you notice **minor finishing issues (paint, fittings, alignment),** note them down.
    - Most reputable developers have a **handover team** to address any last-minute touch-ups before possession.

Pro Tip: Doing a thorough walkthrough **before signing the possession letter** ensures that any adjustments can be made quickly by the developer's team.

Common Mistakes to Avoid

- Skipping the walkthrough and assuming everything will be perfect.
- Not checking utilities and later realizing water or electricity isn't connected.

- Overlooking minor finishing issues—these are **easier to fix before possession.**
- Ignoring **common areas and parking spaces**—make sure they meet your expectations.

Mini Checklist: Before Accepting Your Keys

- Have you tested **all electrical and plumbing fixtures?**
- Is your home **ventilated and well-lit?**
- Are your **utility meters installed and working?**
- Have you received your **handover documents and legal papers?**
- Have you confirmed that any minor touch-ups will be completed?

Final Thought: Your **developer has ensured quality, transparency, and timely delivery**—the final walkthrough is your chance to verify and celebrate this milestone. With everything in place, you can now step into your new home with **confidence and excitement.**

Welcome to Homeownership!

You did it! You navigated the process, made informed decisions, and secured a **valuable asset for your future.**

Your home isn't just a place to live—it's a foundation for security, stability, and growth. Whether it's your first home or an upgrade, this is a major achievement.

Want to Stay Updated on Real Estate Trends & Smart Buyer Insights?

√ Join our **exclusive home buyer's community**—get expert insights, updates, and special offers.

√ Scan the QR code below to **connect with professionals** who can guide you on property investment, home upgrades, and more!

Chapter - 12

SEALING THE DEAL – THE FINAL PAYMENT & POSSESSION PROCESS

The Last Step Before You Get Your Keys

You're almost there. Your dream home is ready. The excitement is real. But before you make the final payment and step into homeownership, there's a structured process in place—one that ensures everything goes smoothly for both **you and the developer**.

This chapter is your **roadmap to possession**. It covers:

√ How and when to make your final payment.

√ The official possession process—what documents you need.

√ What to expect during the handover from the developer.

√ Common mistakes to avoid in the final step.

A well-organized closing process ensures that you take possession **without delays or stress**, while the developer delivers your home with complete transparency.

Understanding the Final Payment Structure

The last payment isn't just about paying off the remaining balance—it's a carefully structured process ensuring **everything is in order before you get the keys**.

√ **Payment Schedule Confirmation** – Developers provide a final payment breakdown, including any additional charges (maintenance, registration fees, stamp duty).

√ **Completion Certificate (CC) & Occupancy Certificate (OC)** – These legal documents confirm that the project meets all construction and safety standards.

√ **Registration & Stamp Duty Payment** – This legalizes your ownership.

Once these steps are completed, you're officially ready to receive the keys.

Final Possession Process – Step by Step

Receive the Final Payment Invoice

√ The developer will provide a detailed invoice for the final amount due, including maintenance, society formation charges, and statutory costs.

√ Confirm that there are **no pending payments or charges** beyond what was agreed in the sale agreement.

Verify All Legal & Compliance Documents

√ **Completion Certificate (CC)** – Confirms the project's legal compliance.

√ **Occupancy Certificate (OC)** – Confirms that the home is ready for possession and legally approved for occupancy.

√ **Sale Deed** – The final legal document confirming the transfer of ownership to you.

√ **Possession Letter** – Issued by the developer once all dues are cleared.

Conduct Your Final Walkthrough & Inspection

√ Before signing the possession letter, do a final check of the home.

√ If there are any minor adjustments needed, **flag them with the developer immediately**—they will resolve them before you move in.

Register the Property in Your Name

√ Pay the **stamp duty and registration charges** as per state laws.

√ Get the **conveyance deed executed**, ensuring full legal ownership of your home.

Get the Keys & Handover Kit

√ Once all payments and documentation are completed, the developer will hand over:

- The **keys to your home.**
- A **handover kit** including warranty documents, appliance manuals, and society details.
- Contact information for the **maintenance team** and society management.

Congratulations! You Are Now a Homeowner.

Your First Responsibilities as a Homeowner

Register Your Name with the Housing Society

√ Most developers assist in forming a Resident Welfare Association (RWA) or society committee.

√ Once formed, your maintenance payments will go directly to the society instead of the developer.

Set Up Utility Connections in Your Name

√ Transfer the **electricity, water, and gas** accounts into your name.

√ Ensure that maintenance fees are paid on time to **keep common services running smoothly.**

Secure Your Home

√ Install any additional safety measures like **grills, security cameras, or digital locks** if needed.

√ Meet your neighbors and familiarize yourself with the **building security protocols.**

Common Mistakes to Avoid

- **Skipping the final property inspection** – Always check before signing the possession letter.

- **Delaying property registration** – Register your home immediately to **avoid legal complications.**

- **Ignoring maintenance payments** – Staying up to date with your dues ensures seamless society operations.

- **Not verifying ownership documents** – Ensure you receive the **Sale Deed and Occupancy Certificate** before moving in.

Mini Checklist: The Final Possession Process

√ Have you received the **final payment invoice** with a full cost breakdown?

√ Have you verified the **Completion Certificate (CC) &** **Occupancy Certificate (OC)?**

√ Have you completed the **property registration & stamp duty payment?**

√ Have you done your **final property walkthrough?**

√ Have you received the **handover kit & warranty documents?**

√ Have you registered with the **housing society & set up utilities?**

Final Thought: Enjoy the Reward of Smart Home Buying

With all legal and financial processes completed, **you are now the proud owner of a well-planned, legally compliant home.** The journey doesn't end here—it's just the beginning of a new chapter filled with comfort, security, and long-term value.

Join Our Exclusive Homeowners Community!

√ Get **expert tips on home maintenance & society management.**

√ Stay updated on **real estate laws & smart investment opportunities.**

√ Network with other homeowners & property experts.

Scan the QR Code to Join Now!

Chapter - 13

PAY SMART, OWN SMART – WHY TIMELY PAYMENTS MATTER

A Home is a Commitment—And So is Its Payment Plan

Buying a home is one of the most exciting milestones in life. But beyond the excitement, there's a structured financial process that ensures **both you and the developer** stay on track.

Homebuyers often assume that **only builders face penalties for delays**—but under **RERA**, the responsibility works both ways. Just like developers must **deliver on time**, buyers must **pay on time**.

This chapter is about **understanding your payment obligations**, so you can plan ahead, avoid unnecessary penalties, and ensure a stress-free home-buying journey.

1. Payment Schedules – Why They Exist & How They Work

Every home purchase follows a **milestone-based payment plan**, meaning you **don't pay everything upfront**. Instead, your payments are linked to **construction progress**—ensuring that funds are released **only as work is completed**.

Typical Home Payment Schedule

√ **10% at Booking** – Locks in your property.

√ **20% when Foundation is Complete** – Ensures the project is underway.

√ **30% when the Structure Reaches the 5th Floor** – Progress confirmed.

√ **20% when External Plastering is Done** – Final finishing begins.

√ **10% at Possession** – Home is ready for move-in.

This **structured system protects buyers**, ensuring you only pay for work that's been completed.

Pro Tip: Always keep a **buffer fund ready**—construction progress might **move faster** than estimated, and you may need to make payments earlier than expected.

2. Timely Payments: It's the Buyer's Responsibility

What Happens If You Pay Late?

Under **RERA**, developers can **legally charge interest** on late payments—just like banks charge interest on overdue EMIs.

√ **The Penalty Rate is Fair & Transparent** – The same rate that developers pay for delays applies to buyers who miss payments.

√ **Delayed Payments Can Impact Your Ownership** – If multiple payments are missed, developers can **send a default notice** and, in extreme cases, **cancel your allotment**.

√ **Avoid Last-Minute Hassles** – Paying on time keeps your homeownership journey smooth and stress-free.

3. Can Developers Ask for Early Payments?

YES—If Construction Progresses Faster

Many buyers assume that **construction follows a fixed timeline.** But if a developer completes a stage **ahead of schedule,** they have the right to **request payment earlier.**

Example:

The sale agreement states:

√ "25% payment when the structure reaches the 10th floor, estimated in 10 months."

√ But the builder **finishes it in 8 months.**

√ **You now need to pay earlier than expected.**

Why This is Fair: You're not paying extra—just paying based on actual progress.

How to Prepare for This?

√ Always keep funds ready ahead of time.

√ Don't rely on fixed timelines—factor in a 2-month buffer.

√ Check your loan disbursal terms to avoid delays in releasing funds.

4. What Happens If You Default on Payments?

Homebuyers often focus on what happens **if a builder** delays possession, but **few realize the consequences of missing payments.**

√ **Interest on Late Payments** – If you miss an installment, you'll pay interest at the same rate the builder would for delays.

√ **Default Notice** – Repeated late payments lead to an official warning.

√ **Cancellation of Your Allotment** – If payments remain unpaid, the developer has the right to cancel your allotment and refund the balance after deducting cancellation charges.

5. Cancellation Charges – What You Need to Know

If you decide to **back out of the deal**, developers have the right to **deduct a small percentage of the total amount as a cancellation fee.**

How Much Can Developers Deduct?

√ Usually **5-10% of the total property cost.**

√ Some agreements state that **booking amounts are non-refundable.**

√ **RERA protects buyers**—developers cannot keep 100% of your payment.

6. How to Avoid Payment-Related Issues

√ **Ask for a Written Payment Schedule** – Before signing, get clarity on **all due dates and amounts.**

√ **Plan for Faster Payments** – Construction can progress ahead of schedule—always be financially prepared.

√ **Read the Cancellation Policy** – Know the exact **penalty for backing out** before committing.

√ **Ensure Loan Readiness** – If using a **home loan**, confirm that your bank can **disburse funds on time.**

Mini Checklist: Smart Payment Planning

√ Have you received a written **payment schedule?**

√ Do you have a **buffer fund** for early payments?

√ Have you checked **interest rates** for late payments?

√ Do you understand the **cancellation charges** if you back out?

√ Have you confirmed that your bank is **ready to release loan payments on time?**

Common Mistakes to Avoid

- Assuming you always have the full time listed in the schedule.

- Delaying payments thinking "the builder can wait"— they legally don't have to.

- Ignoring the interest clause on late payments.

- Not preparing financially for milestone-based payments.

Final Thought: Paying on Time = A Smooth Home-Buying Journey

Homeownership is a **two-way responsibility**—just like developers must **deliver on time,** buyers must **pay on time.**

√ **Timely payments ensure that your home is delivered smoothly.**

√ **Developers follow structured milestone-based payments for buyer protection.**

√ Understanding the process means no surprises—just a stress-free journey to owning your dream home.

Want Personalized Guidance on Payment Planning?

Join our **exclusive home buyer's community** to get:

√ Expert insights on **home loan disbursals & payment schedules.**

√ **Negotiation tips** to optimize your payment structure.

√ **Legal guidance** on cancellation policies & financial planning.

Scan the QR Code to Join Now!

Chapter - 14

THE FINAL WALKTHROUGH – SECURING A PERFECT MOVE-IN EXPERIENCE

Your Dream Home is Ready—Let's Make Sure Everything is Perfect

After months of planning, paperwork, and anticipation, the moment has finally arrived. Your home is ready for handover, and soon, you'll be stepping into a space that's **100% yours.**

Developers work tirelessly to **deliver homes on schedule,** ensuring that every detail meets high-quality standards. But just like any large-scale project, **a final quality check** ensures everything is exactly as expected.

This isn't about **distrust**—it's about **due diligence. A structured walkthrough** helps identify **minor touch-ups** and ensures your transition from buyer to homeowner is smooth and stress-free.

1. Why the Final Walkthrough Matters

A **final walkthrough** isn't about finding faults—it's about confirming that everything is in order **before you take possession.**

√ It ensures you receive the home exactly as promised.

√ It allows you to flag minor fixes early—before you officially move in.

√ It guarantees a hassle-free transition from the builder to you.

Once you **sign the possession papers**, the responsibility shifts to the society's **Resident Welfare Association (RWA)** or maintenance team. That's why this last step **isn't about finding problems—it's about ensuring perfection.**

2. The 10-Point Final Walkthrough Checklist

1. Walls & Ceilings – Spot Any Last-Minute Fixes

- Ensure walls are **evenly painted** and free from **cracks or damp spots.**

- Run your hand over the surface—any rough patches or bubbles?

Why It Matters: Minor imperfections can be **easily fixed before handover.**

2. Electrical Fittings – Check Everything Works

- Plug in a **phone charger** to confirm that all outlets are functional.

- Test all **light switches**—especially in corners and bathrooms.

Why It Matters: Any small wiring adjustments can be handled immediately.

3. Windows & Doors – Smooth Functionality

- Open and close all **doors and windows**—do they shut properly?
- Check for **smooth alignment**—no sticking or misalignment.

Why It Matters: Well-fitted doors & windows improve energy efficiency and security.

4. Water Supply & Drainage – No Leaks Allowed

- Turn on **all faucets**—is the water pressure strong?
- Flush all **toilets**—do they drain completely?

Why It Matters: Ensuring **smooth water flow** prevents future plumbing issues.

5. Proper Drainage – No Water Logging

- Pour a **bucket of water** in bathrooms and balconies—does it drain properly?
- Sloped flooring ensures **water doesn't collect in corners.**

Why It Matters: Good drainage prevents **long-term seepage problems.**

6. Water & Electricity Meters – Confirm Setup

- Are **meters installed and functional?**
- Ensure there are **no pending utility bills** from the previous cycle.

Why It Matters: Having **utilities fully set up** makes move-in effortless.

7. Flooring – Ensure a Solid Foundation

- Walk **barefoot** across the floor—any **hollow sounds** under tiles?

- Look for **cracks or uneven surfaces** in rooms and balconies.

Why It Matters: A well-laid floor ensures **longevity and stability.**

8. Kitchen – Double-Check Cabinets & Plumbing

- If cabinets are **pre-installed**, open and close them.
- Run **sink water**—check for **leaks or blockages.**

Why It Matters: Small fixes are best handled before moving in.

9. Common Areas & Parking – Verify Allocations

- Is your **allotted parking space** clearly marked?
- Test the **elevators**—are they running smoothly?

Why It Matters: Parking disputes and elevator issues are **better sorted before moving in.**

10. Get a Snag List from the Builder

- Request an **official list of any pending minor fixes.**
- Ensure the builder provides a **written deadline for touch-ups.**

Why It Matters: A **snag list** ensures **minor adjustments** are completed efficiently.

3. The Handover Process – What to Expect

A **well-organized developer** ensures a smooth **handover experience**, providing you with:

√ **A comprehensive possession kit** (including manuals, warranties, and emergency contacts).

√ A **structured walkthrough** with the builder or site engineer.

√ A **final checklist** to ensure your home meets all expectations.

What Happens Next?

- Once you've completed the walkthrough:

- **The builder documents any pending fixes** and provides a **timeline for completion.**

- **You sign the possession papers**—officially becoming the owner!

- **The Resident Welfare Association (RWA) takes over**— managing maintenance and common area upkeep.

Pro Tip: Take photos of **your final walkthrough** for personal reference.

4. The Role of the Developer in a Smooth Possession

Great developers don't just **build homes**—they ensure a **seamless transition** for every homeowner. That's why leading developers:

√ **Encourage** buyers to do a thorough final walkthrough.

√ **Provide structured checklists** to ensure nothing is overlooked.

√ **Address minor touch-ups** before possession, so you move in worry-free.

Why This Matters: Developers take pride in their projects—ensuring you get a high-quality home **without last-minute surprises.**

5. Common Myths About Final Walkthroughs

"It's a new home—there's nothing to check."

√ Even **brand-new homes** might need **final touch-ups**—better to check early.

"I can fix small issues myself later."

√ Minor fixes **are best handled by the builder** before possession.

"If I don't point out issues now, I can flag them later."

√ After possession, responsibility shifts to the **maintenance team**—so it's better to finalize fixes now.

6. Mini Checklist: The Perfect Possession Handover

√ Have you verified **all room finishes** (walls, ceilings, floors)?

√ Have you **tested all electrical outlets** and **checked the water flow?**

√ Have you **confirmed your parking spot** and **common area access?**

√ Have you **received a warranty manual** for fittings and appliances?

√ Have you **documented any pending fixes** with a written timeline?

7. Final Thought: Move In With Confidence

Your home is ready, and **your journey as a homeowner begins today.**

√ **A thorough walkthrough** ensures a flawless move-in experience.

√ Your developer is committed to delivering a high-quality home.

√ Taking a few extra steps now means years of hassle-free living.

By taking the time to **review everything before possession**, you ensure that your home is **exactly as promised**—ready for you to move in and enjoy.

Want Expert Guidance for a Smooth Move-In?

Join our **exclusive home buyers' community** for:

- Expert walkthrough tips
- Move-in checklists & legal guidance
- Direct access to real estate professionals

Scan the QR Code to Join Now!

Chapter - 15

LIFE AFTER POSSESSION – MAKING THE MOST OF YOUR NEW HOME

Your Developer is Still Your Partner in Homeownership

Congratulations! You now own your dream home. The papers are signed, the keys are in your hands, and you're ready to move in. But here's something most homebuyers don't realize:

The developer's role doesn't end at possession—it evolves.

A well-reputed developer ensures that homeowners **transition smoothly into their new space**—not just by handing over a house, but by ensuring **quality living, ongoing support, and long-term value.**

This chapter is about what happens **after** you move in. How do you ensure that your new home **remains problem-free**, that your society is well-managed, and that you get the full benefits of homeownership?

Let's break it down.

1. The Role of the Developer After Possession

A professional developer doesn't just build homes—they **build communities**. Here's what to expect from a developer post-possession:

1.1. Defect Liability & Maintenance Support

Under **RERA regulations**, developers are responsible for fixing any **structural defects, plumbing, or electrical issues for up to 5 years** after possession.

√ If you notice minor issues like **paint touch-ups, uneven fittings, or finishing defects**, the developer should arrange for quick rectifications.

√ Report any issues **in writing** to the customer service team so they can schedule necessary repairs.

Tip: Developers often conduct a **post-handover quality audit**—make sure you attend this and highlight any concerns.

1.2. Completion Certificates & Legal Documentation

Before you move in, your developer should provide the necessary legal paperwork, including:

√ **Completion Certificate (CC):** Confirms that the building complies with all regulations.

√ **Occupancy Certificate (OC):** Proves that the property is legally fit for residents to occupy.

√ **Final Payment Acknowledgment:** Confirms all dues have been settled.

√ **Society Formation Documents:** Details on how the community's management will be structured.

Why This Matters: Without these documents, you may face delays in **utility connections, resale, or applying for loans in the future.**

1.3. Society Formation & Maintenance Handovers

Initially, the developer **manages the property's maintenance** until the **Resident Welfare Association (RWA) or Apartment Owners' Association (AOA) is formed.**

√ Expect the developer to provide a **detailed financial report** on maintenance costs.

√ The **RWA takes over after a majority of homeowners move in**, ensuring a seamless transition.

Tip: Attend your **first society meetings**—this is where crucial decisions on maintenance fees, security, and future upgrades are made.

1.4. Warranty & Servicing for Fixtures & Amenities

Your home includes **fixtures, plumbing, electrical setups, elevators, and security systems**—all of which come with warranties.

√ Get a **list of warranties** for installed appliances and fittings.

√ Ask about **AMC (Annual Maintenance Contracts)** for lifts, generators, and water systems.

Why This Matters: Knowing **warranty timelines** ensures that any necessary repairs are covered by the developer or manufacturer.

2. How to Ensure a Smooth Post-Possession Experience

A well-managed real estate project ensures that you **don't have to chase the developer for solutions**. Here's how you can ensure your post-possession experience is stress-free:

2.1. Stay Connected with the Developer's Customer Support

Good developers have a **Customer Relationship Management (CRM) team** that handles post-possession queries.

√ Keep a **direct contact number or email** for reporting concerns.

√ If you need clarifications on **maintenance costs, documentation, or warranty claims**, reach out to the CRM team first.

Tip: If your builder has an **online portal** for tracking post-sale support, use it for faster resolutions.

2.2. Join Your Homebuyer's Community

Many new homeowners **form WhatsApp or Telegram groups** to discuss post-possession experiences, share insights, and track pending work.

√ **Collective feedback** can help the developer prioritize certain fixes.

√ This also helps in **RWA formation and better community management**.

Tip: Connect with neighbors early—this helps in **setting up security, maintenance schedules, and community policies**.

2.3. Keep a Record of Post-Possession Fixes

If you spot minor fixes needed in your home, document them.

√ Take **photos and videos** before reporting issues.

√ Submit requests in **writing via email** to ensure they are formally recorded.

Tip: Developers often provide a **30-90 day window** for minor fixes—use this time wisely!

3. Common Mistakes Homebuyers Make After Possession

Assuming the builder is no longer responsible after key handover.

Fact: The developer is responsible for defect liability for up to 5 years under RERA.

Not collecting final legal documents (CC, OC, property tax details).

Fact: Without these, applying for home loans or resale later can become difficult.

Not keeping records of maintenance charges & society setup.

Fact: Always get a **written breakdown of maintenance fees** before signing.

Skipping the final warranty check for fittings and electrical work.

Fact: Knowing **which items are under warranty** saves you from paying for repairs out of pocket.

4. Mini Checklist: What to Verify After Possession

√ Have you received **all legal documents** (Completion Certificate, Occupancy Certificate, Final Payment Receipts)?

√ Do you have **a contact for post-possession support** from the developer?

√ Is the **maintenance handover plan clear**, and do you know when the RWA will take over?

√ Have you **documented any post-possession fixes** that need to be completed?

√ Have you **collected warranty details** for appliances, elevators, and fittings?

5. Final Thought: Owning a Home is a Long-Term Commitment—And Your Developer is Part of It

Buying a home isn't just a transaction—it's a **lifelong investment.**

A **good developer stands by their project** long after possession, ensuring that homeowners **feel supported, secure, and satisfied.**

When you understand what to expect **after** possession, you move in with confidence—knowing that your home isn't just well-built, but well-managed.

Want Expert Guidance on Post-Possession Queries?

√ Join our **exclusive home buyers' community** to get:

- Insider insights on maintenance & society management

- Post-possession checklist & legal guidance

- Direct access to real estate professionals for expert advice

Scan the QR Code to Join Now!

Chapter - 16

YOUR HOME-BUYING STRATEGY – GO SOLO OR GET A GUIDE?

Buying a Home: The Smart Way vs. The Hard Way

Congratulations! You now understand home buying better than most people. You know the **checklists, legal must-haves, negotiation tactics, and smart financial planning strategies.**

But **knowing** and **doing** are two different things.

Now comes the real decision:

√ Do you **go solo**, handle everything yourself, and navigate the process on your own?

√ Or do you **work with experts** who can guide you, eliminate guesswork, and ensure a stress-free home-buying experience?

There's no right or wrong answer—just what works best for **you**. Let's break down your options.

OPTION 1: GOING SOLO – IF YOU WANT COMPLETE CONTROL

Many buyers prefer to **take charge of the process—** researching, negotiating, and handling everything themselves.

This route requires **time, patience, and confidence.**

What You'll Need to Do On Your Own

√ **Market Research:** You'll need to track property price trends, future developments, and investment potential.

√ **Property Inspections:** Visiting multiple sites, checking quality, comparing pros & cons.

√ **Negotiation Skills:** Handling price discussions with developers or sellers.

√ **Legal & Documentation Review:** Reading every clause in your agreement, ensuring there are no loopholes.

√ **Home Loan & Financial Planning:** Managing bank paperwork, EMI structuring, and cost breakdowns.

√ **Possession & Post-Sale Support:** Handling registration, maintenance setup, and builder coordination for final fixes.

Pro Tip: If you're going solo, make sure you have an **experienced lawyer** and a **trusted home loan advisor** to double-check paperwork and financing.

Is This the Right Path for You?

√ You enjoy **research and details**—you love going deep into market trends and legalities.

√ You have the **time and patience** to visit multiple properties and compare options.

√ You're confident negotiating directly with builders and agents.

√ You have experience in **real estate, finance, or legal contracts.**

Warning: Going solo is rewarding, but it can also be exhausting. If you miss something important—like an unfair contract clause or a hidden construction flaw—it could **cost you lakhs** later.

OPTION 2: GETTING EXPERT GUIDANCE – IF YOU WANT A SMARTER, FASTER JOURNEY

Buying a home is a **major financial and emotional decision.** Having **a team of experts** can remove the stress, speed up the process, and ensure you make **the best choice without the guesswork.**

How Experts Can Help You Buy Smarter

√ **Market Insights:** Professionals know **where prices are rising, which areas offer the best returns, and what hidden gems exist.**

√ **Pre-Vetted Properties:** No wasting time on misleading listings—get access to **curated, high-quality options** that fit your budget and lifestyle.

√ **Negotiation Power:** Developers are more flexible when they see an experienced professional representing you. You could save **lakhs** just by having the right person in your corner.

√ **Legal Protection:** Lawyers and advisors **scan every clause** in your agreement, protecting you from hidden risks.

√ **Financing Made Easy:** Experts help you **choose the best home loan,** structure EMIs wisely, and even **negotiate better interest rates.**

√ ✓ **Hassle-Free Possession**: From getting documents in order to managing post-sale fixes, an expert ensures you move in smoothly.

Is This the Right Path for You?

√ You want **zero stress**—you'd rather let an expert handle the complex details.

√ You have a **busy schedule** and don't want to spend months comparing properties.

√ You want to **avoid hidden risks** and make sure every document is airtight.

√ You prefer a **structured, step-by-step process** with someone guiding you.

Reality Check: Professional guidance isn't just for "first-time buyers." Even seasoned investors rely on expert insights to **find the best deals, negotiate smarter, and ensure risk-free purchases.**

Final Thought: Smart Buyers Buy with Strategy

Buying a home isn't just about picking a property—it's about making the right financial decision.

√ If you love research and control, DIY might work for you.

√ If you prefer efficiency, expert insights, and risk-free buying, professional guidance is the way to go.

Want to Buy Smarter, Faster, and with Zero Stress?

We've helped hundreds of buyers find the perfect home, negotiate better deals, and avoid costly mistakes.

Schedule a free consultation—no pressure, just real talk about your home-buying goals.

Scan the QR Code to Book a Call & Get Expert Guidance Today!

THE ULTIMATE HOME-BUYING CHECKLIST

Your Final Tool for a Smart, Stress-Free Purchase

This is it. The **final tool in your arsenal**—everything you've learned, distilled into one powerful checklist. Whether you're just starting out or ready to move in, use these **checklists as your personal cheat sheets** to make sure you don't miss a thing.

Pro Tip: Download or print these checklists and use them at every stage of your home-buying journey.

PRE-PURCHASE CHECKLIST (Are You Actually Ready to Buy?)

Before you even start looking at homes, make sure you're **financially and mentally prepared:**

√ Do you have a stable income and emergency savings?

√ Have you checked your **credit score?** (Higher scores = Better loan deals)

√ Do you know how much home you can actually afford? (Not just what the bank tells you)

√ Have you set aside money for the **down payment and hidden costs?**

√ Do you have a **buffer fund** for unexpected expenses?

√ Are you clear on why you're buying? (Investment? Family home? Short-term vs. long-term?)

√ Have you researched the **real estate market** in your target location?

Common Mistake: Buying a home just because "everyone else is doing it" instead of actually being ready.

HOUSE HUNTING CHECKLIST (Finding the Right Property)

Once you start looking at homes, **don't just fall for the hype.** Use this checklist to evaluate each property like a pro:

√ **Location & Connectivity** – Is the commute practical? Are there schools, hospitals, and shops nearby?

√ **Noise & Pollution Levels** – Visit at different times to check noise levels and air quality.

√ **Water & Drainage** – Is there a **24/7 water supply?** Does the area have good drainage during monsoons?

√ **Amenities & Maintenance** – Are the promised amenities actually available and well-maintained?

√ **Community & Neighbors** – A great home is only as good as the people around you.

√ **Builder Reputation** – Check **RERA ratings and past project reviews.**

√ **Resale & Appreciation Potential** – If you needed to sell in 5 years, would the property appreciate?

Common Mistake: Falling for **shiny brochures and staged apartments** without checking the **actual property quality.**

LEGAL & PAPERWORK CHECKLIST
(The Must-Have Documents)

The paperwork stage is **where many buyers get scammed.** Make sure you have these verified:

√ **RERA Approval** – Check if the project is officially registered.

√ **Title Deed** – Confirms that the seller **legally owns the property.**

√ **Sale Agreement** – Read every clause. Hidden charges? Completion timeline? Delay penalties?

√ **Encumbrance Certificate** – Confirms there are **no legal disputes or outstanding loans** on the property.

√ **Occupancy Certificate (OC)** – Ensures the property is legally **safe to live in.**

√ **Land Use Approvals** – Verify that the land is officially **designated for residential purposes.**

√ **Home Loan Approval** – If you're taking a loan, ensure all terms and conditions are **clear and in writing.**

Common Mistake: Assuming the builder has **all approvals** without verifying. Always double-check.

FINANCIAL CHECKLIST
(Avoid Hidden Money Traps)

A home's price tag is **just the beginning**—there are additional costs most buyers forget.

√ **Loan Pre-Approval** – Get pre-approved so you **know your budget** before house hunting.

√ **Down Payment** – Have at least **10-20% ready** (or a clear plan for funding it).

√ **Stamp Duty & Registration** – Factor in these **extra legal costs** (usually 5-7% of the property price).

√ **Legal Fees** – Set aside ₹25,000 - ₹50,000 for **lawyer verification and processing fees.**

√ **GST (for under-construction homes)** – Check the applicable **rate (usually 5-12%).**

√ **Home Insurance** – Protect your investment from fire, theft, or natural disasters.

√ **Maintenance Charges** – Get **clarity on monthly fees** before signing.

Common Mistake: Forgetting about hidden costs like interiors, security deposits, and move-in expenses.

CLOSING & MOVE-IN CHECKLIST
(Final Step Before You Celebrate!)

Before you **sign possession papers** and get your keys, do a final check:

√ **Final Walkthrough** – Inspect the home for **defects** before taking possession.

√ **Check Electrical & Plumbing** – Flip **every switch,** test **every tap,** and flush **every toilet.**

√ **Verify Parking & Amenities** – Make sure you're getting **exactly what was promised.**

√ **Utility Setup** – Ensure electricity, water, and gas connections are **transferred to your name.**

√ **Collect Warranties & Manuals** – ACs, water heaters, and elevators—get all guarantee documents.

√ **Hire Professional Movers** – Avoid **last-minute moving chaos.**

√ **Update Important Contacts** – Change your address for banks, IDs, and subscriptions.

Common Mistake: Signing possession papers **before** checking the home one last time.

FINAL THOUGHT: BUY WITH CONFIDENCE, MOVE IN WITH PEACE OF MIND

This **Ultimate Home-Buying Checklist** is your **secret weapon** to making sure you don't miss anything. Use it at every stage, stay informed, and **never rush the process.**

Want to Buy Smarter & Get Expert Guidance?

Join our **exclusive home buyer's community** for:

- Insider tips from real estate professionals.
- Expert advice on documentation & legalities.
- Updates on new projects & investment opportunities.

Scan the QR Code Below to Join the Buyer's Network!

FINAL THOUGHTS

Home Buying is a Power Move – If Done Right

Most people **dream** of owning a home. They scroll through real estate listings, imagine sipping coffee on their balcony, and tell themselves, "Someday, I'll buy my dream home."

But here's the truth: **Most people never actually do it.** They wait. They overanalyze. They listen to those who say, "It's not the right time" or "Just rent, it's easier."

And before they know it, **years pass. Prices rise. Their savings get spent elsewhere.** And that "someday" dream? It stays just that—a dream.

But you're different.

You made it to the end of this book. That means you're serious about home buying. And that puts you ahead of **90% of people** who will never take action.

The Real Value of Owning a Home

Buying a home isn't just about **having a place to live**—it's about securing your future. **It's a power move.** A well-planned home purchase means:

√ **Building wealth automatically** – Every EMI you pay builds YOUR property, not your landlord's.

√ **Stability & control** – No more moving because your landlord increased rent or sold the house.

√ **A forced savings plan** – A home loan makes you save by turning rent payments into asset-building.

√ **Financial freedom** – Once your home loan is paid off, you live rent-free, with a solid asset in hand.

But let's be clear: **Not all home purchases are smart purchases.**

That's why you've read this book—to **avoid the traps, pick the right property, and make sure your home is a true asset, not a liability.**

Avoiding Buyer's Remorse & Owning It Like a Pro

You know what sucks? **Regret.**

When it comes to home buying, regret usually comes in two forms:

Mistake #1: Buying the Wrong Home

This happens when people **rush the process**—ignoring research, falling for marketing hype, or choosing a home that doesn't actually fit their needs.

Mistake #2: Waiting Too Long

Some people keep **"thinking about it"** until prices go up, interest rates change, or someone else grabs their dream home.

Let's make sure **that's NOT you.**

Here's how to **own your decision with confidence:**

1. Get Clear on Your "Why"

Buying a home is a **financial decision**—but it's also an **emotional one.**

Ask yourself:

- **Am I buying for the right reasons?** (Not just because society says I should.)
- **Does this home fit my long-term goals?**
- **Is this the right time for ME?**

The only wrong reason to buy is doing it just because you feel **pressured.** The right reason? **Because it makes sense for you.**

2. Follow the Checklists & Do the Work

If you've read this book, you now have **every tool you need.**

- Follow the **home-buying checklists.**
- **Ask the right questions.**
- **Verify everything before signing.**

Home buying is a marathon, not a sprint. Rushing leads to regret. **Patience leads to the perfect home.**

3. Think Long-Term, Not Just Right Now

The home you buy today should **serve you for years to come.** Look beyond just location and price—think about:

How is the area developing?

Will the home fit your family or career in 5–10 years? Does it have good resale potential?

A well-chosen home serves you today AND builds your future.

4. **Trust the Process & Take Action**

   If you're waiting for **absolute certainty**, you'll **wait forever.** There will always be **some doubts, some nerves, some risk.**

   But by following what you've learned, you're making an **informed decision**—not an impulsive one.

   √ **Trust yourself.**

   √ **Trust the work you've put in.**

   √ **And most importantly—TAKE ACTION.**

   Waiting indefinitely **is also a decision**—a decision to let opportunity pass you by.

□□□□□

THE NEXT STEP IS YOURS

If you've made it this far, **congratulations**—you've done more than most people ever will.

But **knowledge alone won't change your life.**

Action will.

Whether you're actively looking, planning finances, or still weighing your options, one thing is clear:

The best home buyers stay informed, stay connected, and make smart moves.

Want to make your next move with confidence?

Join Our Exclusive Home Buyer's Community!

√ Get **expert insights** & real-time market updates.

√ Learn **insider tips** to negotiate the best deal.

√ Connect with professionals who can **guide you every step of the way.**

Scan the QR Code Below & Take the Next Step!

OR 08585904504